BASIL the BEAGLE

Basil Ruins Christmas

Written by Dawn Wright

Illustrated by Ryan Jones

Additional artwork by Tilly Alexander

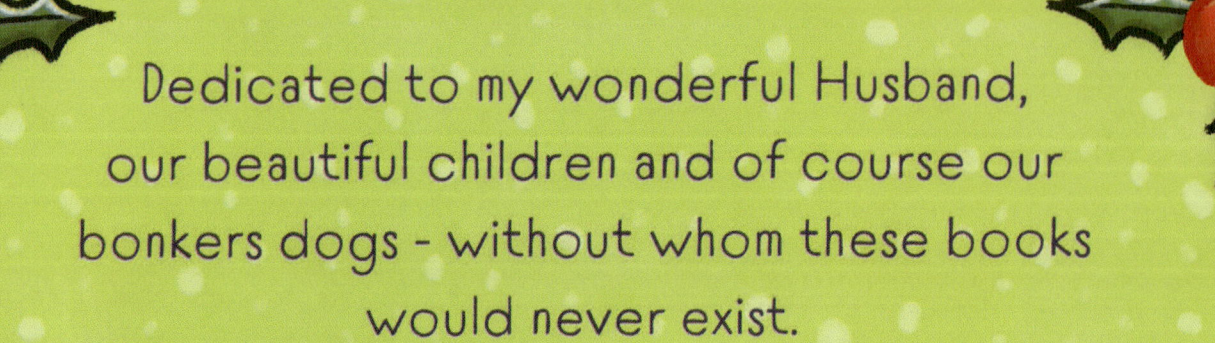

Dedicated to my wonderful Husband, our beautiful children and of course our bonkers dogs - without whom these books would never exist.

This Book Belongs to

_____

First published in 2023
Text copyright © Dawn Wright
Illustrations copyright © Ryan Jones
Additional illustrations copyright © Tilly Alexander

All rights reserved.

No part of this publication may be reproduced, or transmitted in any form, or by any means, electrical, mechanical, photocopying, recording or otherwise without the written permission of the publishers.

ISBN: 9798867771249

Do you want to play hide and seek with Darcy? See if you can find Darcy 20 times throughout the book as you read about a very adventurous Christmas.

Oh look, here she is now! That's your first Darcy. Good luck finding the rest!

It was Christmas eve.

Basil and Darcy were curled up by the nice warm fire as everyone in the Wright family was excited for Santa to arrive!

Ollie and Jazzie bounced and bopped around the room, Mummy still had lots to do, and Daddy... well Daddy had to rest his eyes for 5 minutes, the fun of Christmas is always exhausting – Mummy and Daddy's bank account found it draining too.

2

Mummy helped Ollie and Jazzie put the milk out for Santa - 'it must be such thirsty work for him' thought Basil! Then they put out the carrots for his magical reindeers - with Daddy's help of course.

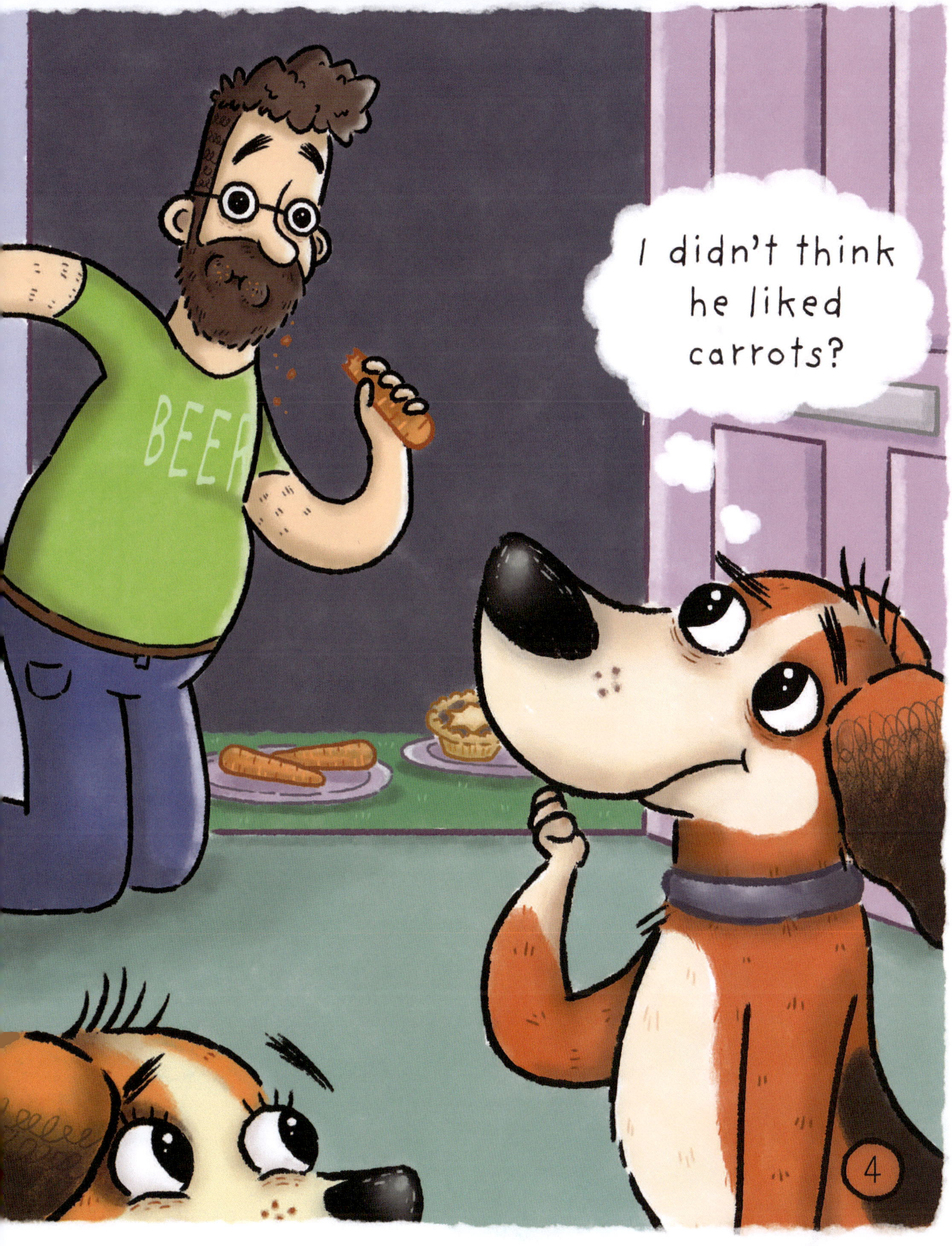
I didn't think he liked carrots?
BEER

"Time for bed" said Mummy, "up the stairs to Bedfordshire - we all want to be up early for Santa don't we?" Ollie and Jazzie were still very excited, but knew the earlier they went to bed, the sooner it would be Christmas!

"Mummy and Daddy are looking forward to an early night too" said Mummy as she lead the children up stairs. It was then that Daddy suddenly sat up, eyes wide open and skipped upstairs - 'I've never seen him so happy' thought Basil.

6

It was very early the next morning - so early the birds weren't even out to sing yet, and Ollie and Jazzie burst into Mummy and Daddy's room - "It's Christmas!!"

Basil followed them in and as
Mummy and Daddy both stretched and yawned,
he could tell they were both so happy to be
woken up as nice and early as this.

With excited screams and shouts, down the stairs they clambered and all stood in front of the Christmas tree. They had all had sooo much fun decorating it together the month before, with such team work Mummy thought.
Basil had watched them have so much fun hanging the pretty red and gold baubles, wrapping the tinsel and sparkly white lights... and now, underneath, were lots and lots of presents from Santa.

It even looked like Basil might have something!

10

Mummy had set the Christmas table with crackers, little presents, knives, forks, spoons and glasses ready for the best Christmas lunch the Wrights had ever had.

Ollie picked up one of the crackers and gave it a little shake, "I wonder what present I will get" he said. "I hope I get a little packet of screwdrivers" Mummy said,
"they come in so handy for making toys".
Daddy didn't look too sure, Basil thought.

Basil was getting very hungry seeing all the food that was getting ready. The plump turkey was ready to be cooked, all the vegetables, roast potatoes, pigs in blankets and everyone's favourite... the annual Brussel sprouts were all prepared ready for everyone to enjoy later.

As Basil began to dream of the dinner to come, Nanny arrived. Nanny absolutely loved a Brussel sprout, but Basil could always smell something funny from Nanny when she ate them.

Before lunch, it was time for presents! Mummy and Daddy thoroughly enjoyed all the noise of cheers and screams that came from the present opening, Basil loved to play with the wrapping paper and Darcy liked to sit and watch what arrived just in case it was anything she could eat.

Ollie got a bike, his first beautiful blue bike - he couldn't wait for Daddy to set it up so he could learn how to ride it and practice absolutely every single day. Basil could see Daddy was just as excited.

Jazzie got a doll, a lovely doll with long hair that she could comb and she could decorate it the way she wanted with her colouring pens. Basil could see Mummy was looking a little worried about Jazzie decorating the walls in the same way - but Jazzie was a good girl and knew not to do that. Darcy got a big fat bone, 'it's nearly as big as me' thought Basil.

And Basil - Basil got something very exciting indeed. Mummy unwrapped the wrapping paper, and out rolled a shiny, round new ball.
I'll call you 'Bounce' thought Basil, 'you're my new favourite toy'.

Lunchtime came, which Basil thought Mummy and Daddy looked very happy about, and they thought it would be a good idea to visit their favourite place - the nice, warm, friendly place where they had grape juice and apple juice with all of their friends.

"Why don't we try your new bike out Ollie" said Mummy, "We'll have a little walk before we eat".

So as Mummy, Daddy, Nanny and the children went off for a walk, Basil, Darcy and 'Bounce' the ball we're left home alone. And it wasn't long before everything went wrong.

Basil bounced and bounced with his new best toy.

He bounced it round the kitchen...

...he bounced it down the stairs...

...and as he made the biggest bounce of all in the living room...

…It flew right into the Christmas tree! 'Noooo' thought Basil, jumping after 'Bounce' and trying to stop him. But instead, he got tied up in the tinsel and the beautiful tree came crashing down to the ground.

'What have I done?' thought Basil, surrounded by smashed red and gold baubles and broken white lights.

'You're going to be in so much trouble' thought Darcy.

22

The family came home to see Basil with 'Bounce' in his mouth, covered in tinsel, and the mess that he had caused. "Naughty Basil" said Mummy. Basil felt sorry, he didn't mean to, he just got over excited. But Mummy seemed to understand, she was in a jolly mood and didn't want to ruin the day. So Daddy put the tree back up and Mummy put her apron on to dish up Christmas lunch.

24

Everybody sat at the table in their usual places ready to eat. They were all so hungry and excited for the big meal ahead. Basil could see the carrots on the table and the sprouts right by Nanny. The smell of the turkey drifted out of the oven as Mummy bent down to pull it out. But as Basil looked over, he saw 'Bounce' the ball... it had rolled right in front of the oven!

26

'Oh no' Basil thought, 'Bounce' is in the way!'
He leapt towards the kitchen, hoping to get
'Bounce' out of Mummy's way in time...
but he was too late.

Mummy stood up with the freshly cooked turkey, turned and tripped, throwing the turkey and all the trimmings all over the floor.

"Naughty Basil" said Mummy. She was much more cross this time, as Basil stood again with 'Bounce' in his mouth looking sorry. "I'm going to throw that ball away if you're not more careful!"

So Mummy, Daddy, Nanny and the children picked at what was left from their Christmas lunch, as Basil and 'Bounce' sat in the naughty corner. "At least we still have the Brussel sprouts" said Nanny.

"Cheer up everyone" Mummy said, "let's play a board game!" Everybody sat up and smiled again - including Daddy, who loved playing games. They cleared the table and set up their favourite one.

30

Daddy knew the rules so well, so he was trying to teach Nanny how to play. The children were taking it very seriously and really wanted to win. "Winning isn't everything" said Mummy, "Just enjoy playing".

Basil was sad, sat in the naughty corner looking over at them all having fun. He didn't mean to wreck the tree, or ruin the dinner.

'It was 'Bounce's' fault', he thought. 'If it hadn't have bounced so hard or got in Mummy's way, none of this would have happened'. He wasn't going to let 'Bounce' ruin Christmas anymore.

Basil looked around to see where 'Bounce' had gone. He couldn't see it in the kitchen, or the dining room.

Then, as he looked up at the table where the family were playing, he could see the rounded top of 'Bounce' in the middle of the game!

'oh no you don't' thought Basil, and - thinking he was doing the right thing - he leapt from the naughty corner up and over the table towards 'Bounce'.

34

As he flew closer and closer towards the table, he could see with horror that it wasn't 'Bounce' at all! It was part of the game that just looked like it... but it was too late.

Basil came thundering onto the table, knocking all of the pieces over, sending cards flying through the air, and was left in the middle of the table with the game board on top of his head.

"Naughty Basil!" said Mummy. She was very angry this time. "What has gotten into you today?!" As Basil looked at Mummy, sad and sorry, he saw out of the corner of his eye…'Bounce', who was sitting in the corner of the room. "I think we need to take away your new toy!" said Daddy, "you've ruined Christmas!"
Basil hung his head and slowly walked back to the naughty corner.

38

The family cleared up the game, and Basil could tell they were all angry at him. He sat and was very sad about what he had done - he had ruined the beautifully decorated Christmas tree, he had ruined the tasty Christmas lunch, and he had ruined the fun family board game. He probably wouldn't be allowed to go on the bog walk later now either - he'd miss running about in the squelchy mud with Darcy.

40

41

As he curled up and tried to forget about it, he felt a hand on his head. Then another, and another, until he looked up and saw the whole family sat around smiling at him.

"We forgive you Basil" said Daddy, "We know you were just over excited" said Mummy, "and at least you didn't ruin the sprouts" said Nanny. "We love you Basil" said the children, and Basil felt warm and happy inside, wagging his tail, surrounded by his family. Darcy wriggled her way through to give him a big lick, and they all sat laughing after a very adventurous Christmas.

The End.

MERRY CHRISTMAS EVERYONE,

LOVE FROM BASIL, BOUNCE AND DARCY.

Next book: The bog walk.

44

Big thank you to Tilly Alexander who also created artwork for Basil.

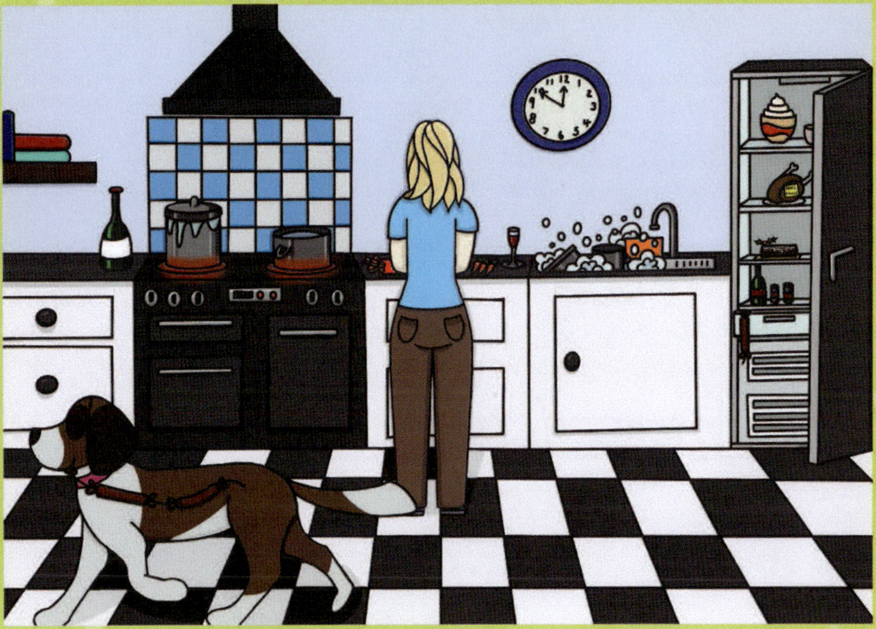

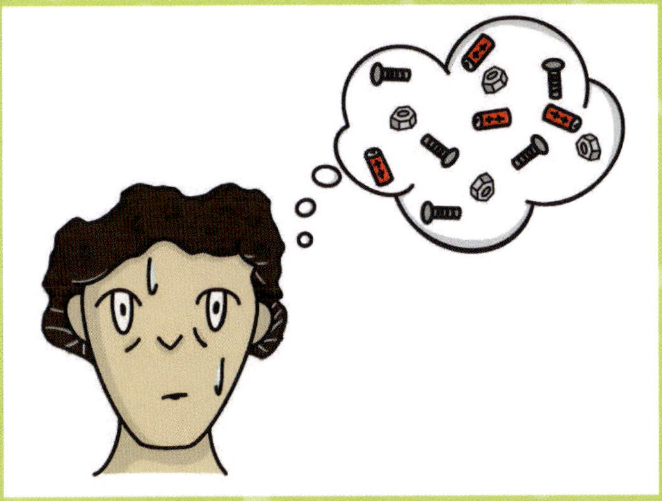

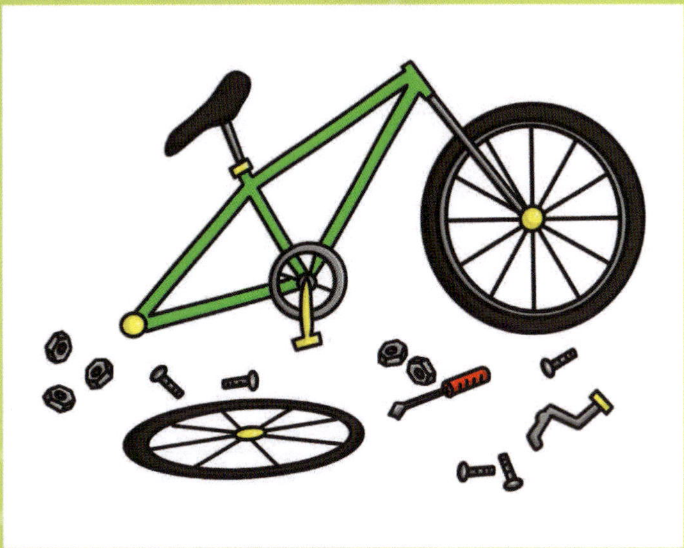

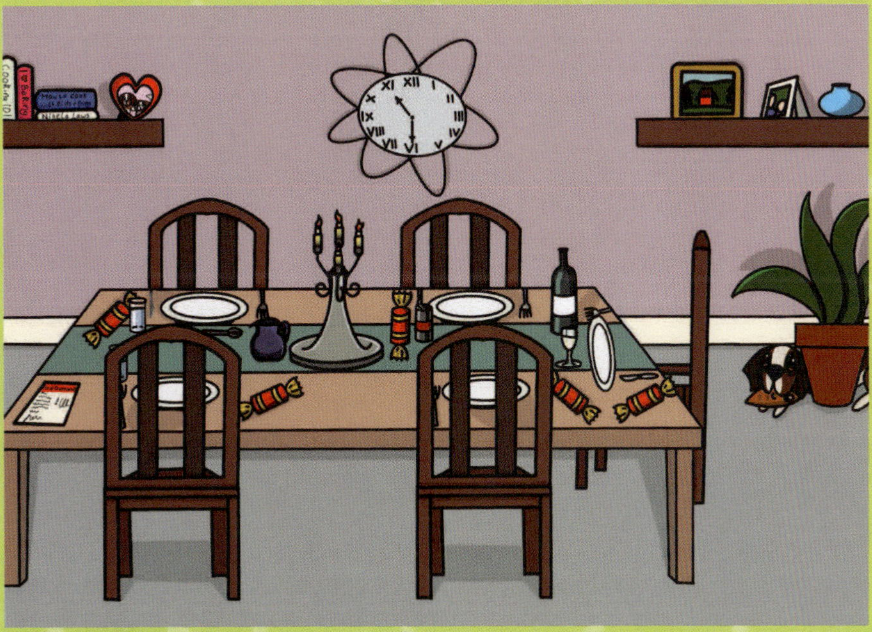

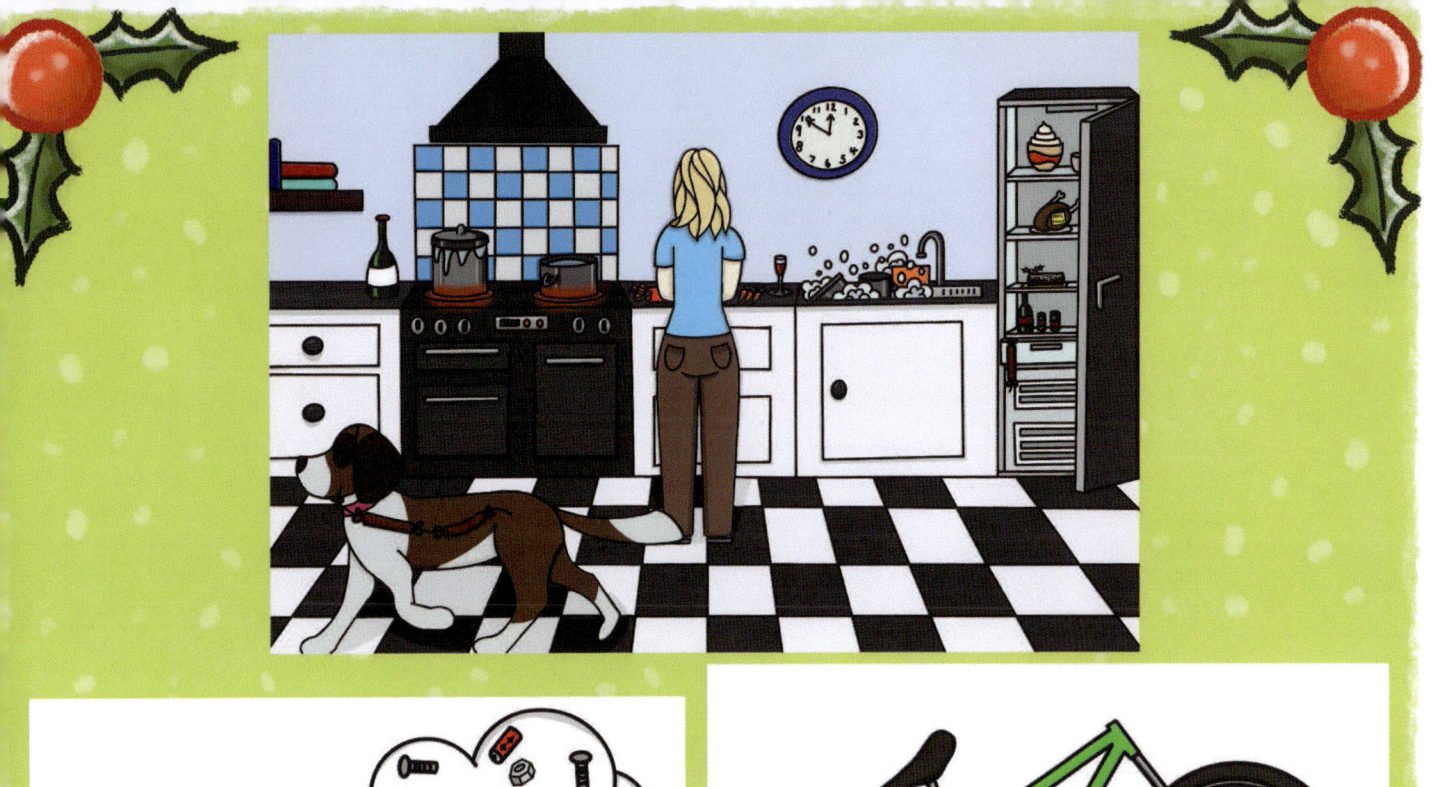

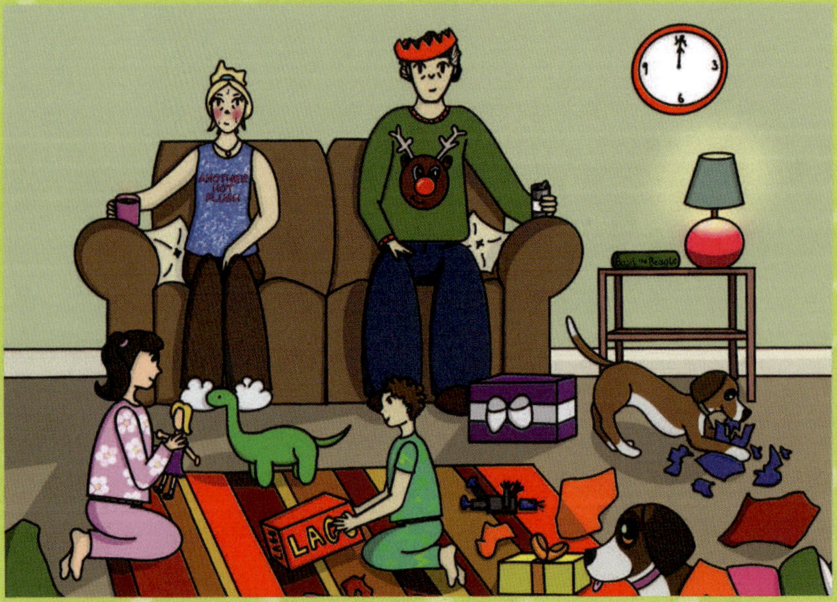

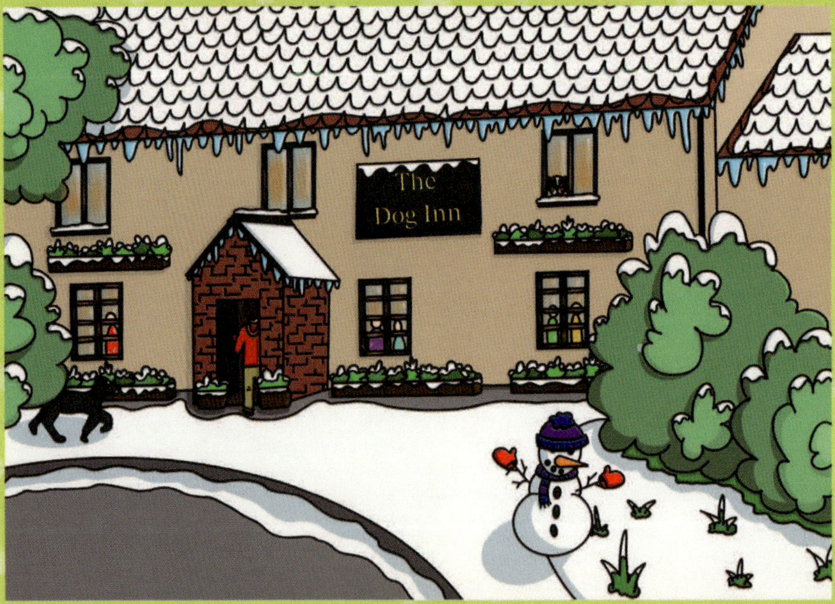
The
Dog Inn

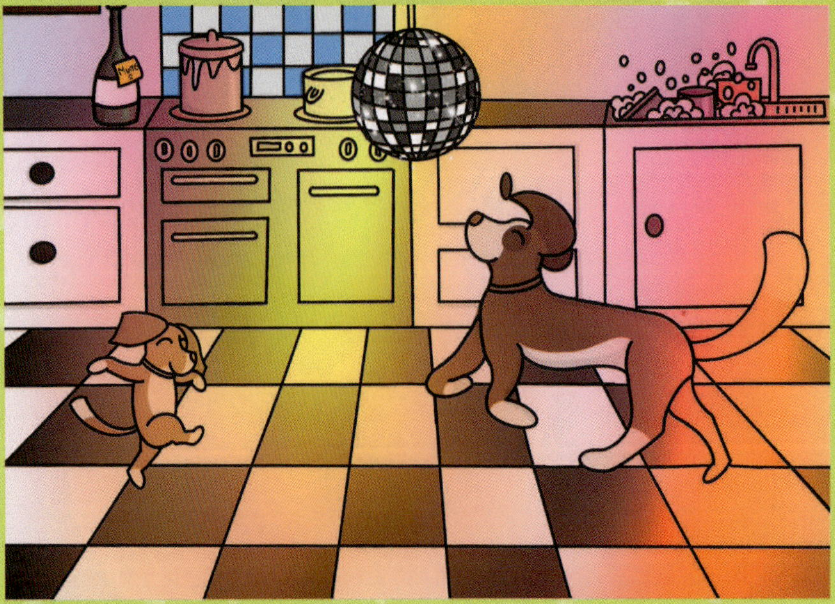

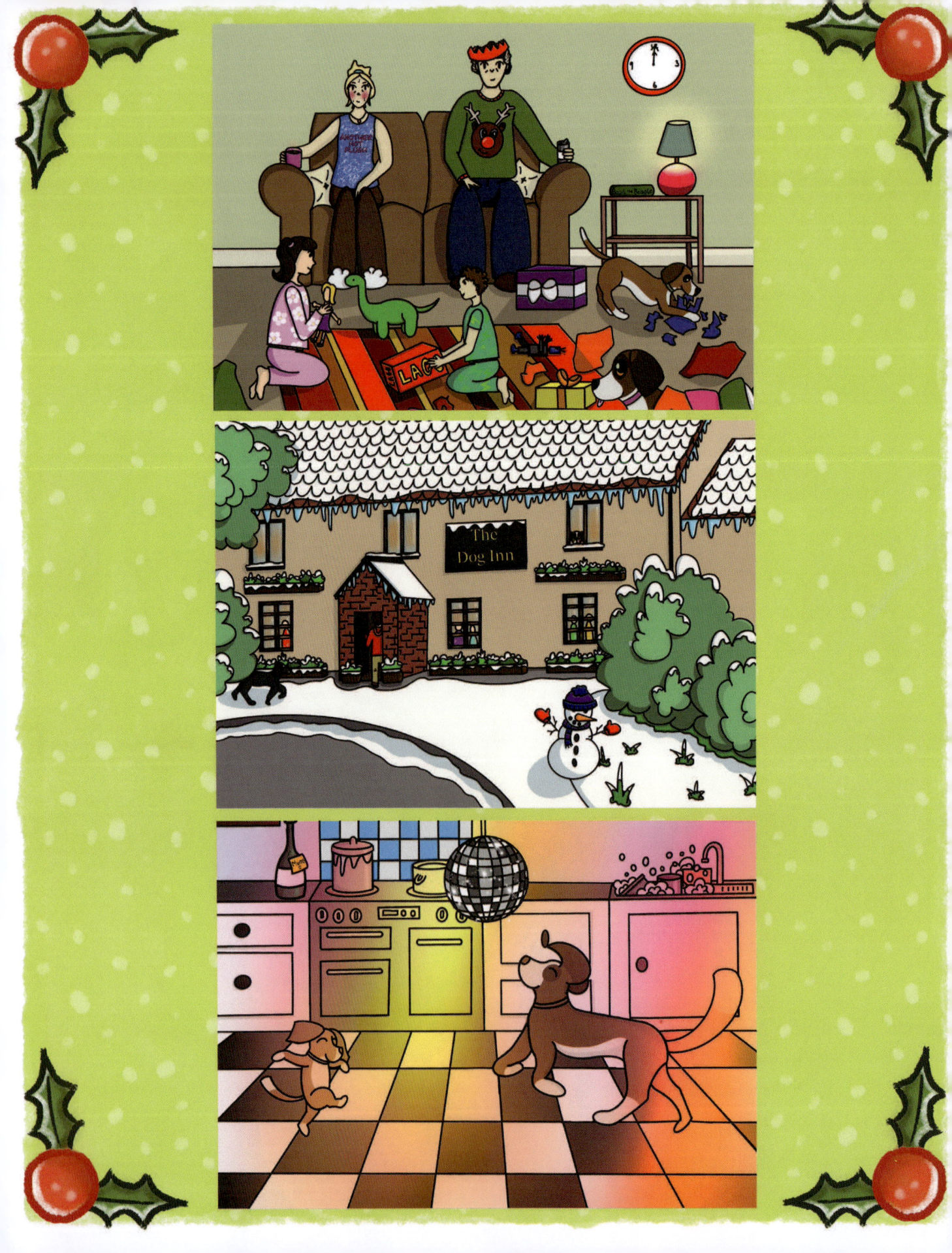

You'r in so much trouble Bazzie boo boo!

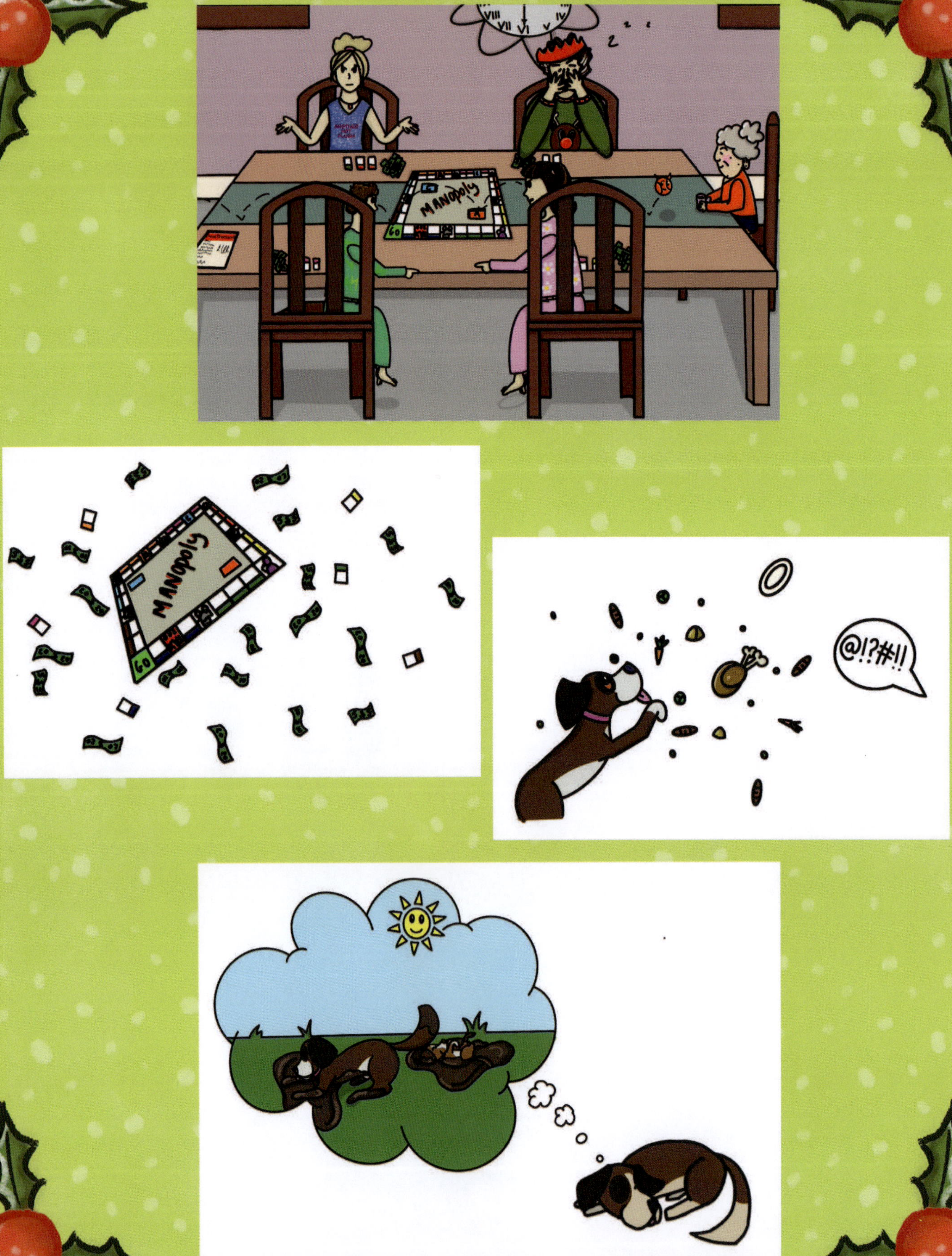
MANopoly
MANopoly
@!?#!!